A Thousand Friends of Rain
New and Selected Poems
1976-1998

A Thousand Friends of Rain

New and Selected Poems
1976-1998

Kim Stafford

Carnegie Mellon University Press
Pittsburgh 2005

Acknowledgements·

Thanks to the editors of the following presses where some of these poems previously appeared in book form: Copper Canyon Press, Confluence Press, lone goose press, and Carnegie Mellon University Press. Thanks also to the editors of the following magazines, where the new poems first appeared: *Northwest Writing Institute Newsletter*, *Oregon Quarterly*, *Ergo*, *Portland Magazine*, and *Harper's*.

"One Prayer from Eden" was performed as the libretto for a choral work composed by Maria Newman at the 1997 Icicle Creek Music Festival, Leavenworth, Washington. "Oregon Reunion of the Rare" first appeared in *Spirit Land*, a limited edition book produced by Margaret Prentice and John Risseeuw. "The Good Son" first appeared in *Writing Path 2: Poetry and Prose from Writers' Conferences*, ed. Michael Pettit (University of Iowa Press, 1996). "A Thousand Friends of Rain" was originally composed for a meeting of the Thousand Friends of Oregon; thanks to Robert Liberty, Director.

This book is for Guthrie.

Library of Congress Control Number: 2005920797
ISBN 0-88748-443-3

A Thousand Friends of Rain was first published
by Carnegie Mellon University Press in 1999

First Classic Contemporaries Edition, 2005

10 9 8 7 6 5 4 3 2 1

The publisher would like to express his gratitude to James Reiss and James W. Hall for their assistance in the production of this volume.

The two adjoining photos on the front lower right of the cover are by Robert Miller; all other photos are courtesy of the author.
Cover design by Adam Atkinson and Dylan Goings

CONTENTS

PLACES & STORIES, 1987

APPLE BOUGH SOLILOQUY, 1995

Naknuwisha

New Poems

NAKNUWISHA

Moon, crow, wind, pine — my friends,
you are my burden, you are my strength.

The bushmen say, "A story is like the wind —
it comes from far away, and you feel it."

On the moonlit dome of Stone Mountain just before dawn,
the wind comes from far away to touch our ears — a crow
calls, and an old pine, patriot to granite, reaches long with a root
to find the crack ice made, and go down deep.

We are climbing to see the sun first look for us, some kind
of prayer. By moonlight, beside my foot, where pine goes
down into stone, I see how the strong thing reaches into the weak place.
Living wood delves into injured stone. Be you with me in the world
like that. Where I am weak, be strong. Where I am foolish, or
paralyzed by grief, be wise in your own way, and feed my grief
with your delight.

Let me tell you how it is: if you sit at the top of Stone Mountain
on the smooth, cold granite dome under the moon, one spark
of mica in the rock will shine for you, small and insistent as a star.
You stare into its silver eye. But then the moon will move, kindle
another mica spark, and then another, and another, stepping its light
across the stone. It is the sun returning from the moon to fire
that little mirror in the earth for you. Let my delight find
some dark place in your story, and yours in mine.

The crow calls, the roots reach down, a story comes
from far away. Before the sun finds us, we need to leave
the single cold we each possess, and gather, as mammals do, in one
warmth — gather my weakness to your power, gather your grief
to my joy. Let us reach like roots toward each other's weaknesses,
saying one to another as the sun comes up,
"Be my burden, be my strength."

DADDY

In that river my blood flowed on.
William Stafford
1914–1993

Rub my thumb in the empty hollow of the milkweed pod.
Daddy, listen me into wind. I close my eyes in the Flint Hills.
Daddy, feed me the old family remedy for homesick: sky,
school, girl, ground, find, storm, home, war, scar, farm.
Daddy, by the clink of flint underfoot, butterfly opens
on coyote scat packed with mouse fur, and by the creek
the long-legged spider carries a lizard tail into the deep
mud shadow of a turtle track.

I reach my hand for what you knew.

Daddy, lead me by bark Braille into the grove at dusk:
honey locust, sycamore, cottonwood, burr oak, catalpa, redbud,
black walnut, Kentucky coffee tree, American elm, red cedar,
red mulberry, hackberry, willow wands in river sand.

Daddy, whisper me home to mangled windmill, Ruby's grave.
Daddy, at the cutbank where the Kaw camped I can almost
smell your smoke, embers sinking low from a hunting fire.
Daddy, where Kansas rhymes with cousin, heartbreak with home,
C.O. with so long, the prairie wind brings you whispering back.

Turn your head and listen to what I say.

Daddy, my willow stick taps our code at the library step,
refinery flame, river bank, at Hutch and El Dorado,
Ninnescah and Wichita, Garden City, Lawrence,
the Sand Hills, every subtle eminence and declivity
in the open country I can find that whispers *Daddy*.

They call it milkweed pod. I call it pharaoh boat, ghost
vagina, moon purse, meadowlark songbag, thumb
pillow, yearning's white mane. Open pod,
the wind gallops away.

Daddy, Comanche's farrier scrawled at the end, "In memory
of old Veteran horse Who Died at 1:30 oclock With the colice
in his stall While I had my hand on his pulse and looking him
in the eye this night long to Be Remembered."

On the prairie alone, I stare into your sky.

They tell me the warriors of the plains valued most the act
of disarming an enemy without injuring him at all, using
the lightest possible weapon. As a feather, you wielded
a hawk's glance, an owl's word — Lame White Man,
Kicking Bear, Hump, One Bull, Crazy Horse, Gall,
Rain in the Face, Crow King, Black Elk, Comes Again,
Iron Hawk, Little Soldier, Sitting Bull, Two Moons,
Law Dog, Bloody Mouth, Hollow Horn Bear.

Daddy, I went out over the prairie seeking you, your
softest voice, and Nietzsche said, "Some persons
are born posthumously."

Daddy, I asked the wrinkled mind of the osage tree,
I asked the glance of shrike, asked the restless
seething spiral of the whip snake cornered in a rut,
asked all that travels over prairie: cottonwood scent,
rain damp, tangle of meadowlark and wind, pungent
colors of prairie grass where the sun goes low.

I went out over the prairie to visit a single tree — faint trail
far through buffalo grass, a few frantic minnows where water
had almost dried. Daddy, in the shade of shocked willow.
Daddy, in flint strata where the flood scoured. Daddy,
on the open land a river through the civilized places
shifts and sustains its own, traveling freely as wind,
as dark, as sky — through static human systems
a thicket of the living wild, just there where the field
ends, the cutbank drops away. Daddy, the raveled
edge of all they have made. Daddy, with my hand through
silk dust, prairie grass, milkweed gone how I found you.

TRYING TO REMEMBER A MIWOK WORD

The boulder by the creek will never forget
what it can do, until it is sand — and then?

The lamb slips through the pen and is free — and then?

Old grandmother oak lies down on the earth, and then
keeps reaching out, each leaf saying "and then, and then?"

I inherit what my parents never did — and then,
what do I do?

        What do I do? I sit on the boulder
by the creek, where Miwok women used to sing.
They have all become quail running down the road
singing like the wind — "and then, and then, and then?"

A Manifesto on Weakness

I have a weakness for the little towns, especially in the early morning
when the first gold light touches sidewalk and storefront in Bucoda,
Coulee Dam, Washougal, Forks, Gray's River, Twisp.
In some sagging trailer on the mountain, where the family left her,
I have a weakness for an old woman trying to tell me secrets
simply because I am younger, and I am listening.
I have a weakness for the dusty sentiments written, carved,
painted, and stitched on the ceiling of the Wishram Tavern,
for the world's largest rosary collection in — where is it? —
Stevenson? I have a weakness for the youngest dancer
in the arena of dust at Nespelem, and the oldest tree
along the bushwhack path of the Duckabush.
I have a weakness for that restless silver thread of water
meeting land around the intuitive margin of Puget Sound.
I have a weakness for a young boy or girl who falls silent
in the middle of the lesson — not because the answer is beyond
her reach, or beyond his grasp, but because the question
recalls the huge complexity of the world.
                                        When the news
is dark, and my own spirit falters, I feel weak and afraid.
But then it's morning, and I have a weakness for mornings,
for my wife and son, my daughter, the tribe of our friends,
and I have a weakness for that impossible, inevitable work
I don't yet know is mine.

ONE PRAYER FROM EDEN

For the woman they called crazy
and left at Spaulding's Rock to starve
near Swan Island, Maine.

At night, I remember the seal eyes looking at me where she perched
in water, blinked and bobbed and stared. At night, I remember
my darling's look, over his shoulder and afraid, closing the door.
The men who rowed me here, and left me loosely tied, who
set me down in fern and struggled quickly into their boat
and pulled away, maybe they hoped I would use the rope
to end it in the pine, to hoist myself and rave and dangle
and be done. But even at the end, it's Eden. Even foaming
at the teeth with cursing, it's heaven where they set me
knowing nothing of this rock but fifty paces end to end,
this tuft of forest rimmed with blue-eyed berry and bloody
leaf. Even at the end it's Eden if it's all you have,
if the only arm you take is a branch, or kiss the dew
from a leaf curl, or gnaw honey bark from featherwood,
or dig thumb roots that taste of soot and salt.
                                        The spreading ripple
from my pebble, echo from my curse or praise, the swell
of my belly stuffed with fern, the brawny wheel of stars, I count
the heart drum in my head when I turn and turn from frost
burrowing into my moss bed frenzy as the night centers into cold.
At dawn, even at the end when I walk the stone circle of low tide,
or stare vacant in my trance past noon, or huddle, hold my knees
in the thorn-stem thicket at evening, the blue light cold, when
the bird cries, "where's your husband, where's your husband?"
When the cricket bickers, "seeding, seeding, seeding, seeding."
When the owl quavers "who be you, who be you?" When the north
wind first fingers through my hair, even then I gnaw through pitch
in a pine-fist deep for seed, taste and swallow wood and mud,
swallow the berry I call *heart bursting open*, the leaf I call
torrent of rain, the seed I call *eyes of my little brother*, the root
I call *woman giving all*.
                                        Sometimes they sit their dory off the point,
two men or three, feather their oars and stare — my matted hair,
my tartan tatters. They shout my name, throw stones. My answer?
I let the bircry to them, the cricket stutter, the wind.

14

I'm through begging. I let them look. I've wept enough. They
must step to my shore now, or leave me. They must find the signals
of their own restraint, if not in my face, then in pine tassel or heron wing
or water shine. To the lost, my Eden seems a place tangled, not tame.
My songs are insect, my doctrine too old and simple to be
understood by book. I settle my thighs on granite, I finger moss.
They sit their dory off the point. I stare and wait, I feel the cold,
I deal in seed and silence, the story in my eyes. I keep this
quiet thing I learned from seal. Stone crack, root mat, stars.

JOULIA'S BOAST

You the biggest ox-bone, seed head, squint-eye,
piss-poor excuse for a man I ever had the misfortune
to endure. You the hero? You the Arnold Wartzenager
of these here back alleys and neon boulevards? If you
the monster man, you the wind-up kind I find broke,
battered, gone into the dumpster back of my burned-out
high-rise poor farm. Mind my own business, say hey?
My business you, poison face. My business to
set you straight about a few details of your fabled
résumé. My business to give you some little shreds
of soul job, as if you might be worthy to advance
along the twisted road from shiny cockroach
you are, to the kind of street-smart big guy you
want to be. Did I say roach? Damn right I did. When I
see your luxury liner Cadillac pull up by my shopping cart
with your mirrored shades flashing and your antennas
wild, you think I don't think roach first thing? Don't I know
you could blow me away so fast it take longer the barrel to cool
than me to die? But I don't think you will. Won't waste me,
sweetheart. You won't, because no matter how fresh you
think you are in that diamond stud rock and wide blue tie,
those silk slacks and blazer bumpy with hid guns as tits
on a boar, you here to listen. Me, I kiss the trees and hear
the bees. You know I pick truth out my gutter like
sweet potatoes in the life garden. I see in your eyes
you hurting for someone talk back to you. That's how you
found me, that's why you asked around and they told you
"Go down to Joulia, go. Go down, don't be sorry." You
won't. You pull up, ease down that window power glide,
I see you. I see three drops coke blood out your nose
on that monogrammed rag you hold. I read these words
you not saying and I know. I say you the child your own life,
you the beginning. I know bird call, I know crow.
I know crow that's hurting when I hear you bark.
Be still, boy child, and listen to me talk to you.
Say hey?

Midnight Literature at the Stardust Motel

Room 3 chain lock torn from the door. . .
Dear Reader, are you ready for Eternity?. . .

and no screen, but a fly swatter
hooked to the wall of cinderblock. . .
Eternity defies man's imagination. . .

through which the non-functioning
cooler looms yellow in the steamy
heat of El Dorado, Kansas, seething. . .
Eternity! — where? — It floats in the air. . .

outside in truck sound and refinery hum —
should I leave the window open and breathe,
or leave it locked for safety and suffocate
in my fitful, smoky, heat-prickled sleep? —
For the wicked this is the most distressing. . .

while here the wall's greasy thumbprints
and brown shag carpet's worn path
lead me across the room to my own
styrofoam cup of rusty water. . .
If a bird would pick up one grain of sand. . .

left on the bedside table where
my smoky pillow gives me view
through the slit of the green
curtain hung from two hooks. . .
*and carry it to the moon, and in that
fashion would eventually carry all of earth away. . .*

to read the label on my wrapped
gift the size of a postage stamp:
"Sweetheart French Milled Complexion Soap."

Eternity would still have just begun. . ..

LOUISE

I went upriver to visit Louise —
stopped at the market to give her a call.
She's always home, working on her beads.
You know Louise.

I knocked on her door, she shuffled me in,
had all her beadwork spread out on a board.
I bought some things, and asked how she was.
She turned away.

I looked out the window to say my good-bye.
The sun was low, the day was cold.
But then Louise started to speak.
I listened to Louise.

She said, "We went down to Phoenix to visit the Pope
that summer when he was there.
I was wearing my red dress that day,
with the white shells on.

My friends they all said they saw me on TV.
They said, 'Louise, did you touch the Man?'
I reached out my hand, but then I was afraid.
I pulled away.

The man beside me shook the Pope's hand.
Then the crowd moved him along.
We got in our truck and started for home,
driving toward Idaho.

As we drove along I was working on my beads.
My fingers shook and I dropped a few.
My little grandson, he laughed, and he said,
'Why do those old things?'

I took his arm and I looked in his eye.
I didn't like what I felt then.
I said some things that I'd say again.
I love that boy.

18

I said, 'It is hard when you sew one bead at a time.
My hands are shaking, my eyes have grown dim.
But are you too lazy, or are you too rich
to sew one bead at a time?'"

Louise was through. I said good-bye,
drove over the bridge at Spalding for home —
on up the canyon, past Kendrick for Troy
as the dark came on.

I went up the switchbacks, out through the pines.
I stopped in the wheat, got out of the car,
stood alone, looked up at the stars
and thought about Louise:

"It is hard when you sew one bead at a time.
My hands are shaking, my eyes have grown dim.
But are you too lazy, or are you too rich
to sew one bead at a time?"

Twelve for Perrin

Wind waits at the door
but when you open
comes inside all at once:
I first heard your name.

In the night
rain strikes the window.
I woke suddenly
to say it.

When you first came to visit
I cut open a pear for us.
Three days later it was
untouched.

My parents gave me what they
could. I can't give back
their gifts. Beloved,
open your hands.

I can't tell my father about you.
I can't tell my brother about you.
All I can do is show you their
crimson paintbrush in the mountains.

Before going away
you said, "My precious."
For a week of wakeful nights
I fed on that delicious crumb.

I lived a long time
without knowing you,
but every evening
the sky filled with color.

Every night alone
I stared at the moon.
You have a way of looking
and not looking away.

The first columbine is single
and blue. I remember
how you said,
"I am afraid."

You put your head
against my head —
the tenderness of wind
just touching tall grass.

In what language
do they name the tree
that stands alone? If you depart
I have been hermit before.

What is portable far from home?
Where does the wind want to be?
I hear the wild geese calling.
Be with me everywhere.

Oregon Reunion of the Rare

1.

I haven't seen our cousin in an age,
our cousin *Summer in a yellow cup*,
our cousin *Turn around and look*.
Some call her Peacock larkspur.
Some call her Applegate's milk-vetch.
Some call her Umpqua mariposa lily.
I call her rare and wild and strange.
Today will I find her at evening
in the swale? Or will this be
the season we say farewell
and begin to forget her quiet ways?

We haven't seen our cousin all summer,
our cousin *Open in the morning*,
our cousin *Many hands in one*.
Some call her Salt marsh bird's beak.
Some call her Malheur Valley fiddleneck.
Some call her Snake River goldenweed.
I call her wife of my childhood.
I call her comfort of my age.
Will she wither all alone?

I went to find my cousin
Trampled by the road's long foot,
my cousin *Drowned behind the dam*,
my cousin *Greed in her absence*.
Some call her Wolf's evening primrose.
Some call her Owyhee clover.
I call her cousin, wife, and saint.
I call her Oregon in small.
Will she survive me, or close
her eyes and slip away?

We can't find our cousin
Silver hands of dew,
our cousin *All we need in grief*.
Some call her Arroyo meadow-foam.

Some call her Pink sandverbena.
I call her smaller than a star.
I call her older than money.
Will she greet us as we walk?
Will she wait for our children?
Will she be rare and wild and strange
even then, when their children
go to seek her in the swale
barefoot at evening?

2.

Have I lost my beloved cousin
Bright eyes in a dark face,
my cousin *Dance on one foot?*
Some call her Coast Range fawn lily.
Others call her smaller than the plan.
Others call her one of many, plain,
and all about the same. I call her my one
child somewhere in the crowd. I call her
my one lit face in the State Fair throng.
How could she forgive me if I lost her?
Would she ever want to come again?

Do you remember our cousin
Open wide for dewfall,
our cousin *Fragrance in the dark?*
Some called her Wayside aster.
Others called her random blur of green.
I call her all created equal.
I call her suffrage of the small.
When we call, will she answer
with that sassy look of hers?

I want to find our cousin
somewhere in the dawn, sporting
the pungent gleam of dew and sun,
our secret cousin *Glimmer of honey*,
our crazy cousin *Wild bee's delight*.

Some call the wild bees gone, their hymns
extinct. Some call the glade still and cold.
Yet I call her and I call her back.
I call our cousins' many names,
who sang the psalms that saved us.

Have we lost our cousins one by one,
our cousin *Starlight on the ground*,
our cousin *Lace of pleasing rain*,
our cousin *Ghost of deep delight?*
Some called her no one knows.
Some called her sunlight magnified
in small and holy ways. Some called her
embroidery on stone by spirit. Vital thread,
here and there she softly trod the earth.
Where now may she softly tread the earth?
Yet in the glen I seek her, bending low.
Will she? Will she be gone? Will she be
our cousin ever again?

August 1997

Our son does not yet have a name.
When he sneezes, he sneezes twice.
He likes to be held high on the chest.
His left leg stretches farther toward the sky.
At dawn on the closed curtain he stares
at the shadow of a moving leaf.
And when he feeds at his mother's breast
a sound comes from his throat that might be
the word in any language for peace, or yearning,
a sound like a boat at night gently tugging at its mooring,
like all the birch leaves at once shivering,
like rain stepping across the clover.

THE GOOD SON

So I'm climbing toward smoke on the fourth floor,
and the boss is still swinging the ladder into place
and I'm already climbing as fast as I can, and I'm
thinking just like I always do on the way up,
"Maybe I'm not cut out for this," but at the same
time I'm noticing the skid tape on the rungs is getting
worn again, and I'm mad at the boss to let the truck get
run down like this, but it's bad to be thinking of anything
but my immediate safety when I get that high—third ladder
section, and they get narrower as you go up—but I always
think of all kinds of things as I climb, I mean it could be my
last thoughts, so why not make them good, and at the same
time I'm curious what I'll see over the top, like is it going to
be someone dead, or passed out smoking in bed, or (like this
one time) these two making love behind closed doors while the
kitchen burns, so you get ready for anything, and about then
I notice the balcony I'm aimed for has the rusted railing about to
fall off, which is true half the time, and the smoke coming out the
window looks yellow, could be toxic, but I also notice this girl
on the balcony to the side, leaning on her railing watching me,
and she's a good looker, and first I notice she's calm, so that
sets me at ease, because my heart still races when I get near the
top, and then through the grating I notice how short her dress is,
and I mean I'm not trying to see it or anything, but I am coming
up from below and it might be my last time ever, since I could be
dead in two minutes if it's bad, and if the boys going up the stair can't
break through the door once I tell them to, some kind of explosion, some
flare-up, and so the girl smiles and I smile, I obey with all I've got, not
wanting anything but that moment, and there's this sweet religion
between us, a whole testament braided in the air just the length
of one breath, but then I'm climbing like mad again, climbing
past her, watching my fingers grab the rungs, and then I'm over
the railing and low in the room and guess what, the smoke is only
six inches down from the ceiling, and there's grandma on the couch
sleeping, and the neighbors banging on the door, and I follow the
smoke into the kitchen and it's nothing but cabbage cinders in a
pot on the stove, so I'm on the radio to the boss with three words,
"*pot au fou*," and he shoots back, "what?" and I say, "everything's

cool," and I'm over and out, but I can't stop thinking of the grandma,
is she okay, and the girl, will she still be there, and so I kill the gas at the
stove, and knock the pan into the sink and smother the burnt cinders of
cabbage, and then I'm padding out to the living room to wake her, and
she's already smiling, she's having a dream through all this, and I see
in the smoky light her face is beautiful when she smiles, and she
must have known some good times, and I can hardly bear to touch her,
to wake her, but she needs some air, so I put my hand on her shoulder
and she opens her eyes, looks up at me and says— "Again?" —but she
can't understand a thing I say, and I know she must be deaf, so she
didn't hear the neighbors pounding or our siren, and I help her to
the window for some air, and then it comes to me we have been here
before, only Pierre climbed last time, and when he found the burnt
cabbage he was so disgusted he wouldn't say a another thing about it,
and I see grandma is fine, the way she coughs and smiles and looks
down as embarrassed as a girl, but not exactly embarrassed, maybe
more like in heaven to have a visitor and all this attention, but I have to
take my leave, not touching the rail, but onto the ladder, and I turn around
and there's the girl, just below me, and I'm climbing down past her,
and as I go by so close I could touch her she asks me if Madame is
okay, and I say yes, and then somebody starts honking—of course
on this narrow street we have traffic backed up everywhere, and
the boss doesn't need the radio with me in view, he's shouting
for me to get down off the ladder if the situation is under control,
and I look at the girl and she's enjoying all the shouting as much as
Madame enjoys the attention, and she's enjoying me, too, and I know
exactly how slow I can go down the ladder to keep the boss under control—
one rung, two—and the old woman is waving from her window, and the girl is
waving from the balcony, and the wind blows her dress and her hair and there's
just a little cabbage smoke, but it's almost gone, and there's just a wisp
of perfume, and the girl's smile is wide open, and I obeyed, feeling it
when she smiled, so I live, and the old lady is so happy I came to visit,
and I'm going down slow—all that honking and shouting on the street,
and I'm thinking, like I always do on the way down—I didn't die, I
didn't even die.

KILLING TIME BEFORE THE NIGHT BEGINS

Recipe say, "Begin with a roux."
I say, what is the roux of my life if not trouble and a song?
At Preservation Hall you close your eyes, the music
    slams through your skin. Stand in the dark, feel the heat,
    listen with your hands and feet.
Out of pain, jazz.
Out of pain — don't kid yourself — more pain.

Guitar man say, "It ain't easy playing with one string."
I say, where excess is the norm, my country first begins.
At the cathedral a lone man stands before the door and sings
            at dawn, "Lord, I be here, I be here."
Out of pain, the blues.
Out of pain — don't kid yourself — more pain.

Cabbie say, "That rag on my aerial? That about my friend
    got killed. He a cabbie. They kill him and they
    steal his money, too."
I say if the Bishop can make it up the stairs, piano be
    smoking tonight.
At the casino, they take your name, shove your money
    down a hole, and the whole palace goes spinning
    down the river so slow you don't know you're gone.
Out of pain, the blue flame at Paddy O'Brien's burns.
Out of pain — don't kid yourself — poor children are born.

Marva say, "Take my husband, but leave my man alone."
Marva say, "When I was born, I brought my daddy bad news."
Marva say, "You look over the whole wide world,
    you never find a woman like me."
I say we be killing time before the night begins, but when
    the night begins, they sell sin cheap on Bourbon Street.
At Cafe du Monde we view the moon.
Jesus spreads his arms in shadow. You know where I mean?
Out of pain: "I went down to St. James Infirmary,
            they told me my baby was dead, dead, dead."
Out of pain — don't kid yourself — jazz.
That's what I said.

A Thousand Friends of Rain

I want to be rain scattering everywhere, licking
   down the long bamboo of a ryegrass stem to the
   dark Oregon earth.

I want to be rain's drum on barn roof and oak leaf,
   on juniper and windshield and salal.

I want to seethe wet into the pungent heart of sage.
   I want to trickle down the eagle's neck.
   I want to blur the ink on a document left outside.
   I want to educate with sensation.

I want to be a filament of Owyhee and Grand Ronde,
   Molalla, Nehalem, and Rogue. I want to throng
   the canyon they call Umpqua, and thunder
   Deschutes to Columbia.

But I want to be the unnamed rivulet, too,
   the silver thread a child finds with fingers
   and tongue. I want to start there, with the
   little ones, and school them to my cause.

I don't want to be a tyrant over my children,
   stealing their world before their hands are
   big enough to touch it gently, leaf by leaf.
   I don't want to tarnish my father's gift,
   my brother's heritage, this place where they
   came home to die. This place must remain.

I want to learn from the sun to be generous, unafraid
   as I spangle over the ghost town of Blitzen.
   I want to learn to love every face and working
   hand, to soothe the convict walking gray in
   the prison yard, and the vagabond seeking not
   a bridge to cross, but to sleep under. Strawberry
   worker bent in the fields, how can I come gently
   to touch your shoulder, *compadre* in our times?

I want to travel through trouble untroubled,
    to plunge down the sewer drain, bubble in
    the dark turmoil of grease and soot, the grief
    and confusion of daily work, and then flow on,
    spread out, rise up clear in mist and return
    to my native ways.

They say Republican and Democrat. I say the
    people of rain. They say cityfolk and
    redneck (my neighbors Alonzo and Sunny).
    I say hospitable tribe of the rain. I say rain
    today in the gray of Portland and the dusty
    green of high desert walking rain. They say for
    and against. I say friend and friend, friend and
    friend in midsummer Oregon rain.

I want to say we look back to Oregon before we
    knew that name — back to cedar canoe,
    to tribal legend and pioneer kerosene lamp,
    we look back to know our story, to know our
    opportunity: we can make an Oregon from
    those same elements of woman and man,
    of child and grandmother, of November night
    by Siuslaw cedar, and midsummer dawn at
    Rowena, of basalt and maple and rain. We can
    make an Oregon that braids the old and the
    not yet known. This is the whole work we do.

So be my dancing partner here. It's all one circle
    by now from gentry to rude mechanical,
    all one spinning world of rain. Vote rain.
    Spend rain. Save and squander rain. Teach
    your children rain. Oregon rain will be
    our shrine, our grotto. I want to ask you into
    the rain, the thousand little hands of rain.

At Kiger Gorge, I want to ask you to stand at
    the rim and listen. At Oneonta, I want to

ask you to remember what you love.
At Perpetua, I want you to tell someone
what you love, but not with words, with what
you do. At Applegate, I want you to witness
for something bigger than the feast of all you
have felt and known. It is there, before you,
at any empty place, where water gleams
in the meadow, and last light touches the
mountain. At Fort Rock, and clear on down
to Hart Mountain I want to ask you to be
in the shine, the chill and dizzy spin of
midsummer Oregon rain today. Be friend.
We have everything to gain. Be native in
the way you take the wet wood hand of rain.

A GYPSY'S HISTORY
OF THE WORLD
Copper Canyon Press 1976

SHAMAN

I hold my hand to the moon
and count the bones.
Then between my fingers each star
is a seed with no husk.
Between my palms is the last
grinding of wheat.

When everyone is asleep I trace
a number with flour on her cheek,
on his foot, and they are gone
by morning.

I go out into the new world,
hear their cries like leaves opening
from a stick. Weed stalks break;
seeds click from the pod; my
shirt like thistledown, I ask
the wind the way: Begin,
begin downwind. I tumble
to the water's edge.

On the river
yesterday's face slides past.
I kneel before the new ripple.

It has taken this long
for my hands
to fill with rain.

COVE

Milk covers the blue flowers
in the china bowl. She lived
alone north of Three-rocks
at the coast. Wind moved
past the chimney: Ave, Ave.

The flowers embroidered on
grandma's night-gown are nearly
worn away. The buttons sewn
with strands of gray hair
are polished like real pearls.
Her name is stitched at the hem
in blue: Eva.

I find this at the Goodwill.

PROPOSAL

The sign for our town
has fallen off the road
into the field.
Wheat gives with the wind.

Bending, the stalks drop seed.
The bearded ears of winter
wheat have their own
whispered song. May our
town's defeat be graceful.

Past where the edge of town was
sit in the wheat and ask
a friend her name. Rain
is coming; don't get up.

YARROW

Rain walks across my back
as I bend to pick yarrow
herb forgotten by the road
waiting for a tired man
who knows the secret

three green leaves between two fingers
crushed   the breath of earth
held before the face   the bowl
of hands surround the taking in
of spirit   yarrow whispers

rain drips from my hatbrim
each hand wears a glove of scent
the road reflects the sky   each
blackbird in the willow hedge
sings praise of yarrow

who knows the secret   a man
waiting by the road   a stalk
of yarrow bending for the rain
I walk across the sky's reflection
convinced by yarrow

Residence in Grizzly

They still own one patch of stony ground
an island of weeds in the miles of wheat.
The last, mute shepherd from the hills,
might come to the porch at Christmas,
his flute taken for a coyote's howl
emerging from the wind.

In winter walking home we listen to each
coyote; surrounding the field of stones
the fence of rust wire hums
like the song we learned
from the people we drove away.

Historic Marker

it was here in mid-winter
they paused to ask each
other the way   the trail
behind filling with snow
> *that broken tree   avalanche*
> *kill   do you remember*
> *late summer   we saw*
> *the break up twenty feet*
> *now here at eye level   deep*
> *snow   bring that day back*
> *speak   are we here*

it was here they built a fire
warmed their hands and faces
until the embers sank
hissed deep in the tunnel
of smoke   here they turned
to look back with the wind
find their tracks nearly gone
then set out uphill   the people
crossing the mountains to find
bitterroot hidden one wealthy day
in a cave on the other side

and here where the wind
slowed just below the summit
they paused to tap out a
song with stiff knuckles
at the base of the last cliff
> *we are here   hungry children*
> *mountain forget   we will remember*
> *wind forget   fill our trail*
> *we will remember   avalanche*
> *be patient   we will disappear*
> *without your help*

it is here   driver   the signs
plastered with snow forget
their names   but you know
the road is endless either way
your car in its brief life
will never fail   the radio
sings what your money can buy

but driver   recall how here
they paused   teeth chattering
a brief prayer   near where
you kneel in the snow
to put on your chains

ORCAS ISLAND

It is surrounded by water
because it is an island.
                                    —Exile

Blackbird dead on the road
raised one wing for the wind
I was walking
                with a scar
on my strongest arm
I came here myself

When wind blows sand   blink
heron with its feet in the ditch
jumps up   flies off
                        the horizon
makes me alone
heart is the only voice
this is one way to keep from being cold

Find a dark place and close your mouth
there is a roof here
I come in where the door hung
once   brambles come in
at a crack in the wall
I take off my hat

Snow has nowhere else to go
falls here   wind brings it in
I scrape straw for a cover
in a corner

In cold weather be cold

BUM

Following his crooked track I
found him under the bridge,
shared a bottle of red,
cottonwood fire.
              Five red lines
made a lady on the wall;
hunters in blue chalk
crouched for the kill.
My friend, knowing the artist, said:
"He never could tell a woman
from lipstick."

Spanish Museum

They were different then, said our guide.
Artists thought they had to be crazy.
Perception possessed them.
This man, he was dying
as he painted this same nude again
and again. She became a nun
when he died. Look at her eyes.
She knew the light of her body
was making him blind.

A Gypsy's History of the World

Before sunrise hides all stars
reach to learn by braille
the single turning constellation
dewfall in the grass
    four-cornered circle spins
    without a sound
    four-cornered circle
    not one made by hand

in sleep a silent bird has
deepest song   a tree's heart still
a flower's rainbow root-held
not to be
    four-cornered circle seems
    right perfect round
    four-cornered circle
    not one made by hand

who owns this restless earth
the nation of the dead and yet
unborn   we who walk here now
take care
    four-cornered circle turns
    all over this dark ground
    four-cornered circle
    not one made by hand

step into the spreading shadow
the cave in what we know
colors are less than the crow
who wears them
    four-cornered circle grows
    in the island mound
    four-cornered circle
    not one made by hand

a leaf remembers its form
seed after seed   with every
constellation of fingertips
a hand recalls the world
 four-cornered circle spins
 without a sound
 four-cornered circle
 not one made by hand

MARRIAGE

Wind-devils spin dust on the slope of sage;
a pale billboard staggers in the gully:
"Graves Hotel — Deep Sleep Guaranteed."
Over the tall, long hills of Montana
we are driving east for a wedding
farther away than we've ever been.
>   *dream alone—*
>   *sleep all night*
>   *then wake the light of day.*

I swerve around a pair of doves
searching the pavement for the perfect
speck of gravel, that bit of earth
that keeps you alive. Blackbird's beak
is a split seed, its song a root all the great
plains deep, our trip a long listening.
>   *red-wing sing—*
>   *for all i've lost,*
>   *for all i've tossed away.*

At the river I gather water in my hat.
It's early yet and Dolly Varden rise,
those supple fish named for the girl who
danced so well in dim light long ago.
I water the steaming engine. Each butterfly
on the radiator grill is courted by a yellowjacket.
>   *dolly varden dance*
>   *but give your answer soon—*
>   *else i'll take that honeymoon alone.*

I think it's someone hitch-hiking, an old man,
trunk bleached white, bark in shreds
hanging to the ground, a single, twisted
limb beckoning. The white line flicks away
like heartbeats racing into the past toward home.
>   *thin white hand—*
>   *where have you been*
>   *now you there in the wind.*

A constellation of white crosses sway
where the guard rail is gone,
a five-cross curve, a family
carried off like sparrows billowing,
the wind's strange custom of remembering,
to touch and move all creatures
in a single turn.
        at graves hotel—
        i'll meet you there
        and we will marry then.

THE BASKET DEEP

The wild honey man is walking on our street.
He listens at the flower places, bramble
trellises, cherry trees broken into bloom
to find the bees and follow them home.

> *From the basket wide and deep,*
> *My Lord,*
> *All seed is cast aside.*

The wild honey man never wears a hat
and sings, his hair thin, coat
patched with holes, yet he's never
stung. He has the quiet eyes.

> *In the summer warm and green,*
> *My Lord,*
> *The pollen all will swarm.*

We followed him once when he
followed the bees. Head in the sky
on the humming nectar path, he'd pause
and listen for the next bee's coming.

> *In the standing field so tall,*
> *My Lord,*
> *By the scythe brought low at last.*

He chased us back that day,
fire in one hand, ax in the other.
His whiskers in the sun glistened
with the last honeycomb he'd chewed.

> *On the threshing floor alone,*
> *My Lord,*
> *Beneath thy flail so long.*

We saw him in the afternoon emerging
from the woods with a pail, brushing
numbed bees out of his hair
so they stuck to his hand.

> *In the winnow wind so high,*
> *My Lord,*
> *All seed that falls is thine.*

The wild honey man is walking on our street,
hive-sweet, tree-handsome. She buys,
standing in her garden humming, tries to offer
him an iris, but cannot break the stem.

> *In the basket wide and deep,*
> *My Lord,*
> *In the basket wide and deep.*

INSIDE THE FENCE:
TULE LAKE INTERNMENT CAMP

The violinist tamed the birds,
fastened branches to the wall,
offered crumbs between his whistling lips.
The children, when it didn't rain,
had to fill a hole with water
so they could see the sky ringed
by earth, their faces wind wrinkled.

Walking was the favorite sport,
finding things, bringing them back
to talk about over tea.
                        We live
this way still, though they say
the war is ended, we can go away.
They took the fences down.
                        Walking
is still the favorite sport, offering
a shoulder to any bird, watching the sky
in a puddle. Our faces wrinkle
for the old days, when we were confined.

EARLY RISER

The home-map glimmers in a swallow's eye,
eager mirror hunting the north star.
Circling constellations stare, an ancestor
flock re-living each night the long circuit,
an old one plunging in a blaze of feathers.

In the rush of its own wind the flyway dips
toward earth, dawn star's declination beckoning.
A globe of dew shows the whole sky
when the beak sips it. With a leaf
for shade each fist of feathers must rest
to rise at dusk, the map of this dark world
in its eye.

BRAIDED APART

with William Stafford
Confluence Press 1976

THE SMALL HOURS

First we learned to dance, then to fly,
then to fall and hide in the grass like quail,
then to creep away low on the earth.

Having that lesson young, we gained
the luck of the old, the knowing about dawn,
the slender promise of a bird.

And this begins the long step into the small hours,
the journey of wind — because crossing
the highest mountain at midnight, midwinter
is safe if you belong to the sky.

While we cling to our path on the world,
footholds on the sheer horizontal face,
we are with the sky, taking in wind
as a traveler for the night, sending it
away again. We are earth that has learned
to breathe, and that is what it means
to dance.

BLOWING DUST OFF THE MAP

A suitor in black, hat filled
with a bouquet of dry weeds,
I'll whistle at the door, then scratch
like a handful of winter wrens
testing soft stone. I thought
you might head north, that's
why I'm knocking, heart
pacing the knuckles. No sound.

Unsure of gravity, mist hesitates
at my shoulder, then dances up
over the house. Half lightning,
half cloud, I would plunge at the road,
having seen your father
in the well-lit depot window
study the schedule in his hands.

Not here, you have escaped into the past,
and I'm holding the weeds, the map
buried in dust in your parents' attic,
generations using this same door,
the film of grime around the knob,
and now two fingers of each
holding most dear a cigarette,
a toothpick, or alone in the field,
a leaf of grass.

CLIMBING THE WILDCAT GRADE

Reflectors along the road, with nothing
of their own to give, await our coming
at fifty to fifty-five. A sign
commands the road to curve
and it curves, the little mirrors
waking dimly at half a mile
to stare, like creatures that would
rush into the path of light.

Aware of stars through the windshield
I turn the wheel in accord with
all signs, the curve of pavement
following the gorge and Wildcat Creek
somewhere below. A path of pear
blossoms covers the road like snow;
we pass the orchard pioneers left behind.

A sign says "Lights" and we are
in the tunnel, concrete corridor
blue with the hum of tungsten globes,
that same cold color of stars.
The sudden, long illumination through
dark mountain makes our faces,
softened by miles after midnight,
alive and afraid. There is no space
between lights, no choice in the
long curve, no escape from what we know.

And when the tunnel ends we enter
the fragile halo of new leaves
surrounding the road, headlights
piercing the mist beyond.
What is that blue cave deepening
into the rearview mirror, as
reflectors ahead wink to life
on the long curve into night.

CROW FEATHER

At the edge of silence
crack your knuckles for luck.
Crow will hear and answer, declare
all shadows created equal,
brothers in black.
                Fingers tangled
as if in prayer, you must agree;
no-one could find fault with stillness,
the universal echo.
                Though
crow insults everyone he meets,
listen for the secret lyric when he
thinks he's alone.

A Story I Remember Hearing That No-one Told

Past the last house at the river
we came to the giant cottonwood
my father meant to climb.
"That hawk nest — I'll see
what's in it."

We watched him tender with
the lowest rotten limbs,
then only careful in the tree's
firm hand, and our feet
clenched to the ground.

He called down, "Nothing!"
and clung there looking our way,
the field below, how we were small
in the nest of grass on earth.

THE GRANARY
Carnegie-Mellon University Press 1982

Rain in the Mountains

Rain comes to earth,
an owl to a mouse in the grass;
the wind enters a budding tree;
a man comes to a woman —
it is the magnetism
of all things.

Brightest leaves fall to water;
water coheres, ice blooms;
the leaves shatter from themselves
at the tiny mouth of the root.

Within the body the body of water
is pulled by the moon, the self drawn
to another integrity, called away,
delight departing, sorrow ebbing
into the sway of a further brilliance.

Snow comes to earth,
a woman to a man —
it is the magnetism
of all things.

A SERMON ON EVE

You know Eve's mother was a man,
and she one bone too many
in his side when he lay numb
and lazy in the summer grass alone?
Down fell the sun on that only
naked man, and stirred within him
then; he slept, and she rose
lovely from the bone, parted
from him for a bride, fair,
full-grown, filled with bewilderment
to be conceived and shaped and so
delivered into flesh. And there
old Adam lay still dreaming on,
stretched foolish, awkward at her feet,
helpless in sleep and solitude, bare
as stone but warm and breathing
like a wave. Sisters and brothers,
when his eyes bloomed wide, and he
looked up for her dark form
against the sun, the plain radiance
of light and shape, of hair
where it glimmered, caused
his mouth to open as he lay
bound within her swaying shadow
of the grass. She looked upon him,
saw the careless sprawl of his limbs
gather, afraid and separate, chilled
by her departure from within
his body's chamber. Her heart was
clenched against returning there —
the air was warm; she stirred, no
longer rooted to him, turned away
yet lingered by. My children, this
is the beginning — how each created thing
knows itself, a single spinning in delight
that then is woven to the world again
and dwells within the garden. Wind
embraced the willow there, and Eve's hair

billowed, and her arms were lifted
in a flame of praise. Old Adam, husk
from which she came, lay stilled
by wonder in the grass, withered
like us all when God the midwife's
sudden hands draw forth and shape
for other purposes the kindled spirit
from our frame that labors at its loss
but then lies quiet and content. Good
people, Eve bowed and gave him breath
again. Peace to you all. Amen.

Red Cloud

Right after the tornado
they drove down the road
to Evelyn's farm: the barn
planks scattered over the field,
the house gone simply — only
the floor, the sewing machine
standing.

There was Evelyn's dress,
thin in the splintered
branches of the cottonwood
where she went through
spinning into the sky,
and there her child
set somehow down
crying in a furrow
halfway to the river.

Taking Anna Home

There was a place on the map
I wanted to be, to be
out in my white coat
where streets carry a name
for miles, and rain trembles down
where you are waiting for it,
and a streetlight holds a place
between all the dark addresses
for a stranger to be resting.
I wanted to be cold and still
to live, to be hungry and
still to live, to be often alone
in search of this, to be
content, not by certain comforts
added to life, but by life itself.
Keep going this way — I will know it
when we find it.

KINDLING

Was it the long valley of my coat
thrown over the bed, or the ragged shoes
waiting by the door to be let out
on their own?

Inside me walked another life,
passive for a time in the wooden
embrace of muscle and gravity,
forgiving for a time the reluctance
of hand, tongue, and eye.
For time would begin
when the air cleared, light
brushed aside, and only
the naked gestures of the hands
leaving the hands behind
set out.

Where I stood
like thistledown when the wind beckons
shed from the body I whirled
out the bone roof in a gown of fire
loving that haggard scaffold
nameless in the doorway.

LA LLORONA

When I went walking by the water early
and mist unfurled the trees before me
and the river was only a sound,
the ground held steady under my feet
until I saw a woman
wavering through the grass, her green
bundle bound in a lace —

    Llorona, ay qué Llorona.

She brought her bundle to the water,
loosed the white cord as one
to another, woman to man,
man to woman. Then
the wrapping of leaves dropped away.
Mist held the trees, and the woman
the pale core of her bundle —

    Llorona, ay qué Llorona.

'Madre de oscuridad, madre
de cielo, madre de tierra,
madre de la soledad. . .'
She saw me in the leaves
and rose as if her bones
wore only a song;
the mist between us cleared —

    Llorona, ay qué Llorona.

She held out her child, a blur
grown small as if receding;
the woman closed her eyes.
I stumbled toward her
in a human way — all I knew.
She parted the bright leaves where
wind made a path in the willows —

    Llorona, ay qué Llorona.

My feet found the hard path again; but
still, since then, in the rain or dark
I've seen her face crumple like a flame
beckoning from the old world where I
lost my way by the water early
and mist unfurled the trees before me
and the river was only a sound.

The Rocking Chair

In the earthquake the rocking chair,
patient so long, begins to move.
In the earthquake, people have no time
for the rocking chair, their shadows
scuttling across the floor, while
the rocking chair takes it easy,
leans back, lets it happen:

the comb thrown down, the dishes
chattering, the mirror flickering
through the air, and birds
leaving the world for good.
But the rocking chair stays
in touch, thoughtful, calm —
a little squeak at the joints
like every afternoon.

When the yard yawns wide, the house
lurching from its crumbling foundation,
and everyone like moles stumbling
suddenly into the daylight, no one
notices the sun crossing the floor
faster than most days,
except the rocking chair
on its smiling feet
dancing alone
in a corner.

Inheritance at Wheatland

A man goes over a barbwire fence,
a child under, and a woman through.
   — East Oregon saying

The yard was fenced to keep horses out,
the barbwire woven with wild rose, but her house
was built without a lock on the door —
an old custom from another time.
With a wave of her hand she gave it all
to the people in town at the end.
They came from Athena for the auction,
from Helix, Ione, La Grande — no one
old enough to know her well.
And when the horses, dressed in leather
and brass, were led away, the obsolete
thresher sold, and all the minor glories
of accumulation in an old family,
childless and done, dispersed, they
had to decide about that house,
the oldest in town, magnificent
in its desolation.

It was unsafe, leaning toward the street
from its blooming grove of locust trees.
There was talk of making it a museum.
'But you can't rebuild the past,'
said the watermelon merchants
to the City Council, and they
were right: 'Preserve what's sound."
So the Fire Department volunteered
to burn it down — a practice run
to train the crew the essentials
of rescue. They'd found a doll
in the attic, wrapped in gingham,
a rude wooden face and hornbeam eyes,
and set her in the round window
niched in the west gable.
Sunday at dawn, without
warning the bell began clanging

and smoke poured from the derelict
cellar, and they all, dressing as they ran
down Main, clustered at the station
to clamber onto the truck howling
up the hill, the long automatic ladder
already lifting as it entered the yard,
the chief with an ax swaying up through smoke
toward that doll hand beckoning behind glass.
But then the roof, tinder dry and shimmering,
blossomed wide; the trees blazed up
in crowns of fire, and the round window
shattered open on a small form dressed in flames.
They pulled the ladder clear, the chief
bundled safe in asbestos boot and glove,
helmet medallion tarnished by the heat
and eyelashes singed away.

But the children arrived in time
to see that face at the eave, that hand
reach out through a veil of sparks
extending a gift of flame
when the house crumbled into itself
within the rows of burning trees.

SLEEPING IN THE BARN

You wake at dawn, snug in the hay.
Warm and steaming, stamping in
through wind the horse comes
storm-weary, eager for oats.
Call this building graceful home:
fog in the field, a wall-board gone,
stall and stanchion long rubbed smooth,
log to post by dovetail tenon,
bale of hay a fragrant table for
tea and bread. Scoop out a
pail of grain from the bin for Rose.
She nibbles the door's old boards.
Invite her in, gently now —
tonight she grazes under the stars.

THE LIGHTHOUSE

You heard about the farm in Dakota
where a single bulb had burned on the porch
for thirty-seven years undimmed,
how people came to look as it burned all day,
all night the landmark on that plain,
went back to their fields to work, to kiss
and sleep, to be born in their homes
all across the land flat as eternity.

They never turned it off,
and children were taught
to walk gently in that house
until they grew and moved away.

There was that light —
then the farm, then Dakota, then winter,
and after dark alone, in pairs or families
the people driving that road would see it
miles away, no matter how late, would make
a little sound under the breath
knowing there was something
other than moonlight
at the core of the human heart.

THE BEARS

My brother saw the amorous bears
rolling about in the meadow up by
Lowder Mountain — the lupine crushed,
paintbrush flattened in their
loving swathe — how he nibbled
her ear and she smacked him
with her paw, there in the fall
of fat September. And my brother
crept away on hands and knees
into the hemlock thicket.
Then the rain, the snow, and we
in our separate lives content
because sunlight struck a pair
of bears apart from our human way —
this wearing of shoes, and words,
and nations.

LETTER TO PHIL

There may be a hoof print or two out
there yet, frozen in the meadow ground,
filling with snow, your gloves by the
splitting maul, the aspen grove you
looked at so long worn smooth by it all.
That reminds me of the song or saying,
'You are burden, you are my strength.'

Moonlit nights you'd appear at the woodpile
in a white robe and slippers. Ax would flash,
snow fly, and any log gleam open at your feet:
ninety year's growth.

'Pleasant words are as a honeycomb —
sweet to the soul, health to the bones.'
And there you were, stomping snow off your boots
till the rafters shook. That night you sang
and paused, and we heard coyotes out across
the meadow linger on a name. A mile or so
of wind went by before you sang again. That's
what spooks horses and cures thieves —
the silence all gone extra deep.

77

CADILLAC

We kept a rabbit named for a car
and a car named for an old woman
while the old woman down the road
kept thirty horses under the cedar trees.
We gave her squash, she gave us manure;
the squash grew thick, honeybees
staggering from the blossom tongues
pollen-covered and a little drunk.
The rabbit sprawled white and drowsy
in the dusky light of the grass,
and the year passed flower
to flower.
                    Trees grew close
together, the blossoms closed by dark.
All things were fragile with us then.
On the shaggy trunk we loved
there was a wound in the wood
that bark closed over and concealed.

PLACES & STORIES
Carnegie Mellon University Press 1987

Bobby Kennedy's Rocker

Up the long rain-aisle of the Hoh
to a patch of firelight, the nightstorm
pounded our three-sided shelter of cedar
carved with names. Hung our packs
on a spike, hung our socks on a line
to smoke, took turns riding a bent-wood
rocking thing of hazel back and forth
as stories went around of work and the road,
of this place and that time, of woman
and man, of hermit and traveler
meeting and departing as water
rattled the kettle to a boil
over the quick flame-swipe.

Midnight, must have been, when a shape
shaggy with rain and bearded like a bear
showed up, would not come close but stood
beyond the flames to point: "It's still here —
no one broke it up for kindling yet."
"Come in!" we said, but
when his hands began to steam
darkness replaced him, a wall of rain
shouting stories for the Hoh.

FEATHER BAG, STICK BAG

This five strands bear hair in a split match,
this about seeing two at love kindle my heart.
How much you pay to hear the rest?

This willow stick red thread tied
be that song before Eve wore shame,
before God pluck the garden key out Adam's
mouth. How much you pay to hear it all?

That ship, mother, go down singing.
You hold feather of the bird that saw,
hold feather of the bird that told me
how they all sang when water closed.
You pay me now, I sing it.

Feather bag, stick bag, this little bone
worry me honest about my people
waiting for me pull the skein of that road
all the way out my fist and be done.
They wait, I sing, you pay, that road
ravel me out.

Dust and water, winter road. Feather
bag, stick bag, bone bag all I had
when dust and water been my food.
Not so always. This blue scrap
be ribbon silk, and wrapped inside
she hides, she laughs my song.
Your money jangle out why.

Feather bag, stick bag — see this
penny my anvil hammer pounded flat?
This the song I sing about you
if you don't buy my songs.

Hah! Feather bag, stick bag, bone bag.

Thomas Jefferson Provides a List of Words So Lewis & Clark May Record the Indian Languages But They Somehow Lose Their Notes After Returning Home

Ask of all local inhabitants you meet
their own peculiar names for these things:

> *yesterday, today, tomorrow, a day, a month, a year,*
> *spring, summer, autumn, winter, a man, a woman.*

Learn these, that future travelers may easily
converse, and that trade may be accomplished
with all fairness and thrift:

> *father, mother, brother, sister, husband, wife,*
> *son, daughter, the body, the head, the hair.*

Note any outstanding appearances of mineral riches
that may obtrude into your sight, and whether these easily
may be worked from the ground and transported thence:

> *redbird, snake, lizard, butterfly, fish, frog,*
> *mulberry, a vine, tobacco, joy, sorrow.*

Record landmarks for bands of settlers who may
follow in your path; note locations of luxurious
pasture, and probable sites of profitable tillage:

> *to eat, to drink, to sleep, to laugh, to cry,*
> *to sing, to whistle, to smell, to hear, to see.*

Observe the natural prospect of the country, that artists
may later depict from certain vantage points
the beauty of this land and people as they now are:

> *to speak, to walk, to run, to stand, to sit,*
> *to lie down, to smoke a pipe, to love, to hate,*
> *to strike, to kill, to dance, to jump, to fall,*
> *to break, to bend, yes, no.*

WILMA TELLS HOW
THEY MOVED OLD JOSEPH'S BONES

They'd planted him first at Wallowa forks
where Nez Perce used to camp, and Old Joseph
he lay there years, sun and snow,
after his kin got driven out.
You been there? Well then you know.
It's always quiet on a north slope
hill. You hear rivers come mix
from west and east.

But then I was a kid running hayfields
crazy all summer when Nez Perce came back
through, and anyone could see
this gravel quarry starting to get made
by where Old Joseph lay under a heap of stone.

It was late September, yes, cottonwood leaves
kicking down at dawn when someone says
Indians gathering at the forks
like old troubles. See any guns? No,
didn't see any. Just their kind of caravan
going south, moving Old Joseph's bones,
looks like. Got him in a buckboard.

They pulled us out of town, the way
we followed those spotted ponies
in the dust, our line of Model-T cars
not wanting to miss out. My daddy
drove first gear all day
those Indians went so slow. No one
said much, except my daddy over his
shoulder once, "Will you look at them?
Will you look? Won't see that
too many times no matter how long
you live" — up past Lostine, past Enterprise,
past Joseph town to the lake, and then
all the horses and cars and us and them
got mixed up, stopping in the afternoon.

There was finding a shovel. There was smoke
and speeches. There was looking at the ground,
and waves hitting on the lake. I was
crazy, I grabbed this tall Indian boy
by the long braids. He pulled me laughing
from my folks between the cars, down under
horses' bellies in deep willow by the water.
He was horse, I was buggy, we didn't know
a word, and I was afraid. I was afraid
to let go.

SHOCKLEY

They called him Briar, he called himself
The Christ, and drove his crimson Cadillac
at ninety up the curves of the cliff road
to Idaho's heart — home the white chapel
where disciples waited for his flaming mouth
to kiss each word away. Madonna was his mute
mother, and Magdalen the city waitress he brought
back to the fold one Sunday dawn to preach
a sermon on. She wiped her tears away
with braids unraveling, was saved
and shouted as he bellowed clear,
"See! See this holy woman raised
from the neon pit of iniquity
below us on the plain, at the far end
of the road I drive. Late last night
I plucked her out from the diner where
she toiled, was coiled in sin,
and brought her up the mountain,
bretheren, to be raised, raised up
to the heights her soul finds capable
with me, by perfecting guidance changed
from what she was to what you see before you
rising, weeping and repentant, purified."

She stayed, she joined, she praised
beyond all others, until word came back
his Cadillac had left the road past midnight
and two brothers brought him wrapped in spotted
white to the vigil of the collect. Three days
they waited, sung out glory. Three nights
they locked the doors, for only their Lord would break them
wide with flaming hands.
                              But then fourth dawn
they took the floorboards up and buried him,
fit the linoleum seamless down, broke
open their church-pod from within,
scattered back to their lives, to wages
and fever, possession and fear — her apron

to some diner, her hands to that seasonal trade
that ends not, her mouth to piecework and words
not sanctified, to the taxes of love for another's
hunger lip to lip.

TUBBY TELLS ABOUT HIS UNCLE MIKE

My uncle rode with the James boys, you
heard, back them days before Jesse's shot,
and Uncle Mike, old fox, dropped the dollars,
give the posse the slip, landed in the mountains.

When I was five and he was beer-soured old
he'd lead, I'd tag along to a shadow
canyon, two big silver sixguns
jangling at his sides. I'd stand

a heart-sized bottle on a stump
at forty feet, then crouch behind his legs
propped wide in fern. He'd shout,
Come out the door you little coward!

then draw, one flash his hand exploding
six times, sudden still, while he'd
reload, clicking six gold shells in
then blast his left gun empty

quiet as the wind.
"How come," I says, "you don't
shoot both guns at once?"
Fire in his eyes, dead fern

withered to his knees: "Tubby,
a man with two empty guns
got as much chance in this old world
as a naked woman on a busy street."

Followed him home where he hung
his guns on a nail, shriveled
into a chair, sang me by firelight,
"I've lived single all my life."

LIBERTY DOLLAR

She was single as new silver, her thin
dress easy. He opened windows for a breeze
and taught her to be dancing but be still.
"Must close your mouth. Hush. Look
through that window: plum tree blossoming,
rain."
         On the dais she was at last
a flame at eighteen chilled to permanence
when he veiled the plaster, put his small
knives away, held out her coat, and she

was gone into America, land of little
mirrors, of one girl calm, a ribbon in her
hair, a year below her face
face-up on the counter, worn smooth,
tarnished, earned, stolen, struck
new in the die, an honest dollar
spent as she grew older.

"I'm sorry," he had called. "Don't
be afraid. You have the face I need,
the face of liberty" — as rain collapsed,
as the tree burst open, as the girl
turned to look.

Her Mother Tells Her

Fine, little Ida. You got both shoes,
all fourteen buttons by yourself. You made
the long blue ribbon straight. This man
makes his camera ready. Winter light shines good
he says this morning. There on your face
his shadow — that's the cold place you feel.
Don't shiver. He doesn't want you shivering.
Play your *kantele*. I will tell you
when to stop.

In our Finland they want to see you
with the *kantele*. Play "Winterleaf"
for Oiva. Play "Little Box."
Play the one you like. I know
the *kantele* is cold. I know.
No use tuning it now. Later we will.

But now be still. With four stones
I prop your rocking chair. There. Now
stop moving your hand. Look up.
Now be still. Be still, little Ida,
be still.

Losing One

Too small to work at haytime
she down by South Fork making
her willow house. At dusk some said
her red ball drifted skittish
too far out. Some said maybe
swimming, maybe sunshine in her eyes.
Some said, now keep her mother home,
now send her father searching far fields.
All women, men, tall children
to seek her body fast at the riffle,
slow through pools, all in a chain
knit hand to hand, at each bank
ankle deep, in the channel to the breast
and gasping at the suck and swirl,
the current burrowing brown from last
night's mountain rain. Swallows dipping,
thunder to the east, not much talk
but *Hold me. Wait. No, nothing.* That
family tribe — sister, cousin, now
brother, father, mother in the line, flat
gray waterslap, not willing ever
to stop. Chill and mosquitoes,
ozone smoke, lightning there
and there, then starlight:
Enough? Not yet. And she
somewhere bumping the long scour
of the riverbed without a word.

FLOWER DRAWN FROM THORN

You took me to the mountains
where we stood among the corn.
You covered my mouth and spoke:

> *little straight tree, beautiful and happy,*
> *not yet turned aside to wisdom.*

You led me higher and I looked again:
your face a tree's wood shattered apart,
a stone the years tore open. My clothing
was a darkness pulled away:

> *little bird, lick water from each bud —*
> *you will be satisfied.*

Stars stood thick above me.
I had not watched our twisted path
for you were leading. Then you left.
There would be no sound. My hands
made knobs of light. I was to be
tamed. You told me this: water
would be ice, and ice clear stone,
and stone the skull protecting God.
The wind passed over. Then
a shape loomed up before me. For this
I rose, and all my trembling fell away
as my clothing had fallen in the corn.
My fingers found the mouth that spoke
and hurt, a blessing from it flowed
over my shoulders, and I fell by
blood into the grass for joy.
Carried like a rag, raised up, I hung
suspended in her arms. One mouth
served us both, one small song
tangled backward through my teeth.
Claws unraveled my fingers, unraveled
my limbs, crumpled my body and
cleared by burning what I knew,

by the fire of stars opened
my moon-bright head of shell
until my eyes looked inward
for the world was done.

Heavy when I woke against earth,
my hand held a bloom of pain
and dark with the red sweat of life,
its work, its grief. Delight went
through me bone by bone. I longed
for water. Then, when light had come,
you found me, knelt down
beside me with a cup and blanket.
I took them so you would not speak.
I stared into your face.

If We Shed Our Names

At the heart of Pocatello ants have built
a city of their own small labor, life by life
jostling thick sand into a mound
to turn away rain from their deep home.

They toil inside the steel fence of the transformer
compound, the Power Company's preserve. No-one
walks beyond the Danger sign, unless they carry
a sprig of food or a belly of water.

By noon sun is on them, by October
snow has covered their pyramid.
Their praise returns in spring.
They grow smaller and older than we.

Within their labyrinth, ancient paradise
the size of a footprint, they retreat into their factory
of earth to practice by sleight of hand and scent
intimate politics with juniper and rain.

SALISH GRAVEYARD, CENTRAL B.C.

When wind flips open her grave-house roof
each hand holds what it owned:
scissors, thimble, sewing machine
wheel that hand wore smooth
still belonging to its cold bones.

All working parts become one,
screws wedded to the steel they held.

Then snow-melt admires metal:
one little shuttle frozen with rust,
its bobbin of black thread sealed inside.

When St. Babylon Rides Her Midnight

Limousine to pick up strangers starved
at the ruby heart of Reno no one pays her
any mind, though she spangle her dress of dimes
spilled from slot machines, and jangle
her pretty voice out the window sliding by.

They turn from the glint in her eyes,
from laughter jostled out those little
lips she paints with moon. St. Babylon
settles back to cruise, tells her husky driver
"One more time down the Avenue, but slow."

About the hour the street-sweeper waggles
at the curb, and cleaning folk shiver
for their busride home, the last hard
figures twisted by dizzy sacraments
of hunger, cross-eyed wine, are propped

or fallen on the steps, or tumbled
flat in alleys under a slit of starlight.
Then they hear St. Babylon stop
her long black ride for the holy
lonely children of the street, hear

her high-heeled slippers step through wine
and shattered glass. Through their delirium
the driver lifts them stiff with cold,
slides them in the back seat easy, that door
closed with a heart-beat snap. She rides

before their startled bodies raised
from their heaps of rags to see
smoldering eyes that snuff out stars,
hair furrowed by rain, and tall bones
bound for distances.

Paulina Rodeo

There was once the fiddle's shriek
and startled cry of a dancing woman's
pleasure, and once the bawl of men calling
each other out — "You Harlan, Roger,
Wade, and Reub, get over here!"

There once was steady thunder
of the bulldogger's horse gone
pounding out the chute, and sun so hot
beer sweats, and hazed steers
balked even crazier than usual.

There once was that fine old buckaroo
guest of honor riding a thin horse slow
around the arena to shake every
grinning man's hand and kiss
every handy woman on the mouth.

But then the roll of night
and chill dawn sudden somewhere
west of Suplee where he took his razor
and red bandanna down to the stream
to shave, and redwing blackbirds chanted

their watery songs, and lupine
glistened out from hoof prints, and water
shattered from his hands as he peered
cold into the steel mirror holding sky
fragrant in a fist of sage.

WHAT EVER HAPPENED
TO STUMPTOWN'S GYPSY SLIM

Who camped under bare library elms
with his saxophone and little stove:
"Excuse me, mam. I have a question
for your time. You see, I am about
to sauté my onion for the evening and I
wonder what herbs you might recommend?"

Shopping cart man who stretched plastic
over that bench carved Laurence Sterne,
eccentric danger from another time,
spoke: "I don't care if it's family, friend,
house, job, creed, ethnic group, country,
institution, or sex — they *all* try to stifle
what *you* can be."

But they got him. Pigeons settle
where his cart kept city pavement dry
a few months, and clean citizens
are not afraid to walk on that side
where his raving once made them stop.

Aunt Charlotte Said

Rosemary, this story my daddy
told me when I was your age: Down
by the caves in the Catskills his father
said to him, "Don't ever go in. Dark
and cave-slime cover your face. You
might never come out, might never
get dragged out. I didn't raise you
for that, to lie in a narrow slot
stuck silent before you're grown."

But then my daddy was a little older
than you. He found a cave, pulled
a tree aside, went in where only he
on hands and knees could slither deeper
on his belly, could hitch along after
the candle's flicker, the plunk of
water somewhere past the tunnel's
bend, breathing all his breath away
deep at the tight place to be
smaller than he was: wispy little
body way down under the cold
rock of the world.
                    The dark opened
in a room. He wiped mud off his eyes,
held the candle up. On the wall
was a word scrawled the way a child
his own age would write: his father's
little name.
                    Oh his daddy's gone, Rosemary.
And my daddy's gone. But I keep that story.
You remember now: there are two names there
in the dark of the cave, way down in the earth
where they were not supposed to go.

This Woman Was Our Kite

When she'd had one too many
we heard a small whippoorwill song
and she lifted off hilarious as fog.
When the tallest branches of the elm
failed to snag her loose hair blaze
and missed the petticoat she swirled,
men stood stunned, and children cried,
"Grandmother! Come back before you break!"
But she smiled mindless as a photograph, lost
her dainty slippers, with dizzy poise
and a laugh spun upside down, her
billowing lace unraveling smaller
as she rose toward evening stars.

A white thread trailed over the grass —
"Grab it! Knot the end so she
can't get away!" Her daughter
knuckled a hasty spool.

Women called out, "Lady reach wide,
trim your sail, don't fall!" Our long
thread tugged at stars and yearned,
wind swung easily around, and she
became a pale trace adrift on silent
constellations of Nebraska's roof.

"Praise the Lord for beauties
of the night!" her sister said.
"Mind of her own and always
had," her husband said. "I'm
letting go," her daughter said.

HACKSAW SAYS THEIR MARRIAGE VOWS

I am the first part of joinery —
this dividing of self from self,
this opening wedge with a kerf
of light in my slender wake.
I take you down by sawdust
fine so you don't miss
those old shapes done away
by the marriage of fire to wood
where one flame speaks.

Salmon River cuts through hills.
There's only one passage now:
my teeth on the blued steel blade
divide all things, reveal all things,
consume all things, renew all things
to what they were before. For even he
must be clean divided from himself,
and she from herself, to become one
passion kindled right.

Book of Hours

For the kindling in his touch, her hand
opens so still bobbing grass not jostled
at all, swaying ripe in her dowry pleasure
turning to her hours of stars, her lit
fingers lifted in praise fevered to serenity:
More and less in the savor they
build intrinsic as bone in me, less

and more where lace-print leaves dyed
my shoulders, less for desire and more
this hour for fear desire would not
come back when called by the bleat
I spoke, when his head a mute
breathing knob rested by mine
and less and more were done.

Stand for pollen, for rain, for each
hour spent, for starlight's
gift, the gift of cold she held
out and he took, for the book he
offered and she read with her lips, her
tongue and his, the book she opened
by starlight braille and he knew.

FIGUREHEAD OF THE GOOD SHIP MARYANNE

Her breasts swell to shatter waves
that hid a battered rose bouquet prayer-snug
between her hips. Twin knees dimple
the wet green dress pressed close by wind,
cedar hem scattered like a catspaw
over two red shoes firm on the prow
carved bountiful with leaves.

Her black hair billows, her face juts out
so bold the cruelest sailor's tempest would
quail for two eyes crooked of a diverse size,
for that red mouth split at a glint of teeth
where laughter soon, soon will blossom.
For the rage of every thousand, thousand
miles be cast in tatters off his back,
and the lamp turned low, her shoulders
unfurled, the night-prayer clenched
in her wood hands revealed, where terror sunk
wells up to foam when the century fathom
blue in her quick eyes lights the deep.

Restless Calligraphy of the Human Form in Boundless Varieties of Change

Because hair is one long garment tethered
to the mind, because she is a flame
they could not quench, because
one life is not enough dance
breaks from the chrysalis
of a woman, all flow, hinge hip
and wrist, pliant as fire where it turns
in its writhing path. Ever logical by varying

she drifts into the open, shimmers
on the narrow stairway music
carves from darkness, her hand's bud
unraveling, arms kindled by a lamp that
blossoms vein by vein, desire rooted
desperately there where the dance
sheds her body stepping wild and gone
like smoke from a long burning,
when the lights go down
and music dances from her
in a separate shape away.

IN A PHOTOGRAPH MY GRANDMOTHER, RE-SHINGLING THE ROOF, PRETENDS TO BE DEPARTING FOR HEAVEN

Wrinkled smile, gloved hands, minister's
bride grips her saw to rip clouds wide
that bar her tight-mouthed path toward stars,
toward blooming gingham, Bible leaves
strewn out, toward their hayhouse honeymoon
again for love beyond sight. She might
with rimless glasses, with that white apron
safety-pinned to her bosom lean
beyond the ladder's last rung,
roof shattered about her, open
rafters studded with nails by that tornado
of one life winnowed husk house.

His sermons, her diary, their silence:
Nebraska wind passionate about ripe
cottonwood stripped and budded. His seed,
their pod, thunder's vine she rides — gone up
her jagged path of light.

Don't Talk on the Sabbath: Sing or Be Still

Its hinges spoke open
where wind came waltzing in,
closing the door behind.

She swayed through the room,
hands clenched on a spoon or prayer,
humming an old hymn: Jacob's Ladder

in the barn, the loft piled high
for a place to lie snug while
winnowed light filled the building

bowing under the seasons swinging
swallows in and out, grandmother
calling from the house

eighteen years away.

Under an Oak in California

When Hitler kissed the children
and Mussolini played the violin
my father planted spindly cork oak
saplings in the dust of California
because they feared this war might
never end. "The nation will need cork
and wood and shade," the foreman said.

He with a crew at an awkward march
over the hills above some snug town
with a saint's name took two steps,
swung his short hoe at the call dividing
earth, and one thin blade of life
from the bag at his belly rooted there,
then the crew lurched forward.

Maybe the rain would come, or maybe
the crew return with water packs.
"Plant many, for many will die," the foreman
said, while Hitler kissed the children
and Mussolini played the violin.

Opening the Book

When our landlord's name was Manlove
and the world was three years old, when the car
wouldn't start and summer was longer than life
and lush with dew, in the soft morning we stepped
early onto the tarred trestle above Tualatin
river water fish nibbled, leaves flashing between
ties aunt Helen counted for two nephews, who were
my brother and me, and then the parents
with the baby between them, singing,
"I feel like a morning star."

On the far side shining grass and shadow
we tumbled into the wild orchard deep
with sunlight and spearmint, opened our
blanket to shake out walnuts and bruised
apples, father in the pear tree calling down
where we were sticky and laughing rolling
late plums into hollows of grass, Helen
pulling down an arc of white roses
so our basket might be filled, mother
humming with bees while my sister slept.

How carefully we walked over the trestle
toward evening, how slow toward winter
and the house that would burn, the strange
changes our bodies would learn and carry
for another sister, for my own child, for dying
and dying and dying all our words poured out,
and trees we would hollow into earth and
pray for shade to cover our family
singing "I feel like a morning star."

After the Barn Collapsed,
Boones Ferry Road

I found the swarm toiling on their comb,
slanted wall slung taut by blackberry rope
rooted to earth. It was May, honeyflow,
and the bees frantic to taste and spit,
to trample, trade mouth to mouth flowersap
their bodies held for such meeting — all women
but the drones' blunt heads bee-women fed
tongue to tongue.
              With smoke and water,
with a leaf-brush I coaxed them
into my white box. The barn would burn,
the place be scraped to raw dirt.
Only a few escaped to finger the wax
print my blade left behind, to hover
where their wall had stood and speak
their buzz twang of despair in the honey month.

ALL

Possession is a weight, physical simply —
all love a second body we feel we need:
woman, husband, daughter, son.

My child, my child I held you simply,
a lump drawn from my weight —
my lovely bloom who from the stem
would go, drifting abrupt from reach
until my hands and body nearly tore
from themselves to take you back,
back, and back.
                    But then I
withered as you grew or died or
disappeared into a stranger
older than the one I shed
(retreating inward, weightless
as a seed).
                    Oh Summer, Autumn,
Susan, Gabriel, May — which
name was it that I chose? Which name
did you become, and live through, and leave
before I saw it carved on stone?

My little oat, awkward as wind in my arms
when I lay you down for sleep, let this be
my saying for you — once you are born,
once you are mine, then free, forgetting
who made this song
that made itself.

WALKING TO THE MAILBOX

We found a turtle stunned by sunlight
dozing easy with half-shut eyes,
and as I bent down, my little Rosemary,
strapped to my back, stirred and
murmured. When I held its knobbed green
body up, her quick breath moistened
my ear, while the turtle, dazed
by eternity, made perfect unto itself
by so many million years, looked
back at my little one, all wisdom
and danger, trouble and delight
unfurled in the slots of its yellow eyes.

Hunched on the ground again it broke
from its trance, sinewy legs
reaching out, the green skull
of itself tottering slowly away,
made strong by wearing its
own death outward, as I did
rising up with Rosemary.

Joanne's Gift

At dawn Joanne heard mule colt
bray and went to feed it. Down
Smith River road a single foxglove
bloom whizzed past, grazing her shoulder
to skid and quiver in the rut. By her
shoe the bruised bloom throbbed, flower
with a black slim stem that buzzed. She
plucked off ragged purple to find
a ruby-throat feather thumb
hummingbird kindle the light
and be gone.

Years later, as she rubbed the grown
mule's ear at dusk, she told us
how these seasons care for her,
how good neighbors leave her wood
and bread, how sweet the taste,
her cup of water.

BACK HOME IN THE SHOPPING CENTER

I found the corner where children ride
the worn plastic horse leaping on its post,
tail adrift, saddle horn dark from desperate sweat,
leather reins jingling with chrome — but now
so still, so still it made me lonely
for a quarter, for a body small enough
to clamber into the gum-studded saddle
tooled with roses, to kick the red spur
so the pony rolls and champs its bit,
runs away, muzak whinnying,
other mothers turning to see
who squalls from that wobbling steed
blasting for the sage. Oh centuries,
you are so little for human joy.

APPLE BOUGH SOLILOQUY

Lone Goose Press 1995

When I was a sapling I rose
from meadow grass, a budded stem.
The second year I divided
and reached outward. I had learned
to believe more than one wish.
You know this opening?

The third year, my blossoms ached
from every twig, and bees came
with their tongues,
their pollen dust that thrilled me.
I shivered. I shed my gown.
The fourth year, two birds wove
me a pocket at the fist where
I centered. Two came, and six left me.
The fifth year, after the bees, after the
petals swirled, after I had dressed
in green, I felt quickened at one fingertip.
One small fruit hung there.
Rain tapped it. Wind swayed me.

The sixth year, my south bough
hung heavy with apples.
A crow called her companions there.
They sat in a row on my thin shoulder,
nibbling from the apples,
and I let that limb down slowly, until
by late summer the farthest twig
nearly combed the grass. Apples fell
in a row, sparkled with frost,
softened into themselves, the earth.
You know how treasures change.
You have seen it.
                    The seventh year
I dressed sturdy in jewels.
I felt my heartwood thicken,
and the apples suckling
everywhere upon me,

the little mouth at the tip
of every stem sipping from me,
and I reveled. When they fell away,
I felt each stem scar close tight.
That winter, I sagged with every limb,
hunched low toward earth.
My apples had bent me,
my giving took me down.

Snow settled
on all my shoulders
and the crows came back,
perching and preening
glistening black,
flexing their heavy bodies
as they tossed their calls
into the wind. I felt old then,
bent. I looked down at my foot.
My roots dreamed through the earth
for a mineral sip, a cold feast.
You know this feast, how
you savor it alone. Then, in my eighth
year, the warm wind came breathing
through, and the rain kiss everywhere.

When sun teased open every bud,
when dew licked every leaf and blossom,
I went up again in a throng of saplings,
spindly wands rising from
the crabbed turmoil of my old self.
The pine had asked me why I ever
bent down, why I should ever falter
from the green urge toward sun.
The oak asked me now,
why this childish rush
of thin ones rising, why not settle
into the kinks and crooks
of my character, and be done.

Oak. You know how friends can be.
Pine, Cedar, Redbud.
My reply to my friends?
My reply took years
of bending down, then rising up,
blossoming again, inviting the tongues
of bees, the sweet sap that fills me.
I replied with great apples
that took me down,
that bent each new youth I managed,
tugged me with each harvest
I gave away, until my humpbacked limbs
showed the rhythm of their making.

Wave upon wave, I staggered
and climbed, bent and rose,
kneeled low in the cold to doze,
and then woke to the bees' clamor.
Others in the grove have said maturity
achieves a single stately shape:
the grand beech massive at the bole,
the elm towering stout into its distant
green shimmer. But I say maturity
endures by blossoming,
by one root feeding both heartwood
trunk and whitewood sapling,
by yielding equally to sun and cold,
to the lift of light and the pull
of apples down.
                        I say yield
to the blaze of leaves that dress
you green, to petals that shimmer
from you, to late summer
yellowing from within.
I say yield to the barren time,
the naked scrawl of yourself
gathering from earth a new thrust.
I say green sapling.

I say bee tongue searching.
I say praise the appleseed that leads us
through such trouble.
I say join me in this festival
of hard change. Forgive yourself
for complexity, for this dance
of bearing and giving away,
extending and standing with
a new poise. Reply to speeches
with action. Bend and rise.
Find pleasure in the
sun-hammered life
that kindles.